All-American
Salt & Pepper Shakers

Sylvia Tompkins & Irene Thornburg

Schiffer Publishing Ltd®
4880 Lower Valley Road, Atglen, PA 19310 USA

Library of Congress Control Number: 2002101041

Designed by John P. Cheek
Cover design by Bruce M. Waters
Type set in Van Dijk/ZapfHumanist BT

ISBN: 0-7643-1618-4
Printed in China
1 2 3 4

Published by Schiffer Publishing Ltd.
4880 Lower Valley Road
Atglen, PA 19310
Phone: (610) 593-1777; Fax: (610) 593-2002
E-mail: Schifferbk@aol.com
Please visit our web site catalog at
www.schifferbooks.com
We are always looking for people to write books on new and related subjects. If you have an idea for a book, please contact us at the above address.

This book may be purchased from the publisher.
Include $3.95 for shipping.
Please try your bookstore first.
You may write for a free catalog.

In Europe, Schiffer books are distributed by
Bushwood Books
6 Marksbury Avenue
Kew Gardens
Surrey TW9 4JF England
Phone: 44 (0) 20 8392 8585
Fax: 44 (0) 20 8392 9876
E-mail: Bushwd@aol.com
Free postage in the UK. Europe: air mail at cost.

Contents

Acknowledgments

We sincerely appreciate the assistance and encouragement of friends and collectors, and especially the following contributors to this book: Diane Bass; Cody Bayne; Barbara Burke, author of *Hull Pottery, The Dinnerware Lines*; Larry Carey; Toni Crittenden and Art Voorhees; Dot Gammon; Bob Gentile; Shirley Gimondo; Marty Grossman; Lorraine Haywood; Verity Hobbs; Betty and Freddie Hunter; Wendy R. Johnston; Heath Karr; Sharon and Ralph Karr; Phil Mays; Jean Moon; Sally Oge; Joanne Rose; Sabra Sattler; Sally and Kurt Sebert; Marcia Smith; Jean Stalder; Karen Weaver.

Introduction

In the beginning, most collectors acquired sets because they were appealing, a souvenir from a trip, received as a gift, or simply because they had holes in the top. Through the years, as collections have grown, their owners have wanted to learn more about the origin and background of various sets.

Interest has been steadily growing in American made salt and pepper shakers, and although books have been written on some American companies, salt and pepper shakers were not the primary focus. We are presenting sets here that are from lesser known manufacturers as well as sets made by familiar companies. Featured are shakers made by Regal China Company, Matthew Adams, Sascha Brastoff, Elbee Art, Shirley and others. We have also discovered a significant number of interesting and unique sets designed and crafted by two California pottery artists in the 1940s, Margaret Weese and Billee Vier.

Values are based on input from contributors and our experience. As always, values are intended only as a guide. They will vary based on condition, geographical location, knowledge of the seller and buyer, and sometimes, pure luck. We found that pricing Regal China sets was especially difficult. Price fluctuations over the past year or two have been caused by Internet auctions and, to some extent, collector interest. Therefore, prices may occasionally vary considerably from those shown.

Plans for our third book on this subject include sets made by Arcadia Ceramics, Treasure Craft, Twin Winton, California Originals, Rick Wisecarver and others.

The Novelty Salt & Pepper Shakers Club is an international organization of 1300 members. These collectors enjoy the friendships and benefits derived from joining with others who share a love of this hobby. Twenty-three regional chapters (twenty-one U.S. and two Canadian) afford an opportunity for collectors to get together with others in their area. Each year the Club convention is held in a different part of the country to give as many members as possible a chance to attend. A special set is commissioned for each convention and is available for purchase by Club members. Quarterly newsletters provide information on shaker identification and history, as well as a means to buy, sell and trade. For more information about the Club, please contact the authors.

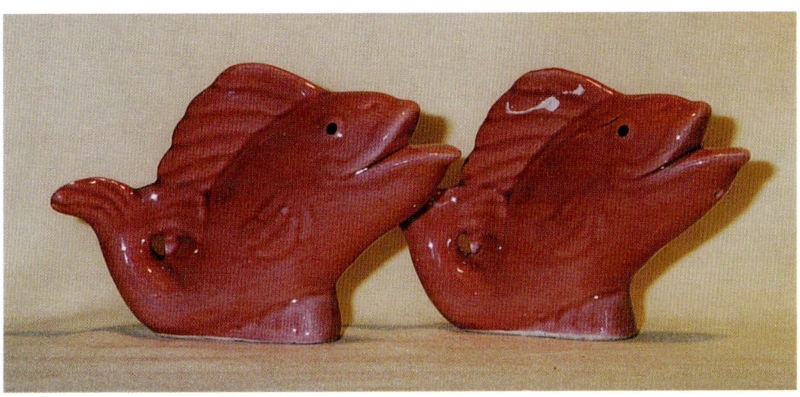

Various Potteries

Regal China Company

Regal China, located in Antioch, Illinois, was founded around 1938. Their main wares were Jim Beam bottles, cookie jars, salt and pepper shakers, and similar novelties. In 1947, production began of the "Snuggle Hugs" or huggies, designed by Ruth Van Tellingen (Bendel). The Old MacDonald series was produced from 1950-1952. Some sets are marked "copyright © C. Miller," who we assume was a designer for Regal. Most of the shakers without accent color contain manufacturing defects. Regal produced the 1991 and 1992 convention sets for the Novelty Salt & Pepper Shakers Club. The 1992 convention set, "Leaf People," was the last production run for the company, as it closed in June 1992.

Note: Two sets with speckled gold trim, the French chefs and Goldilocks, are often thought to be Regal China. Although similar in mold design to Regal, these sets are much lighter weight and usually have a number on the bottom. They were not made by Regal and are shown for information only.

"Snuggle Hugs Series" label.

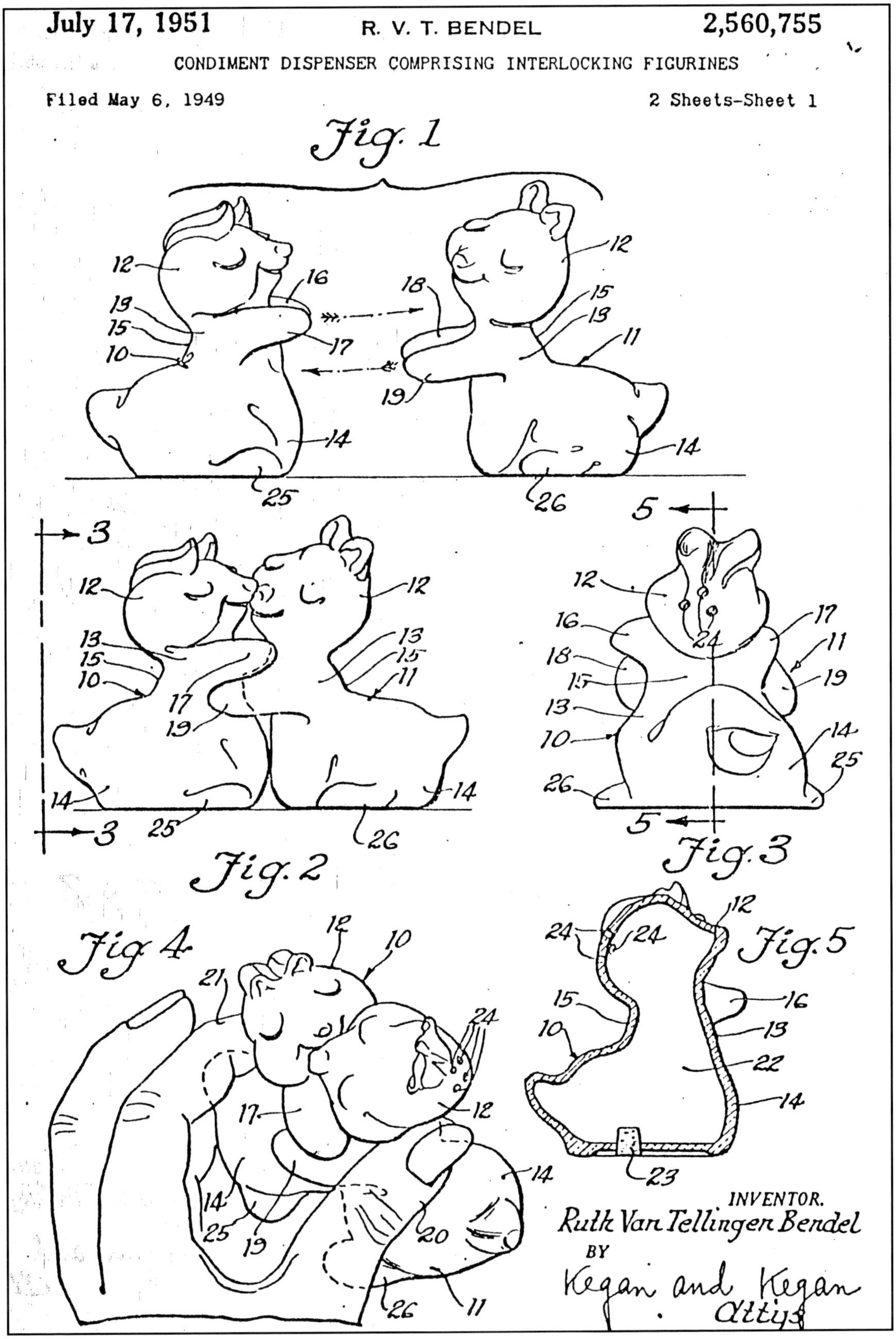

Snuggle Hugs patent application drawing.

Both Pages:
Van Tellingen Bears. 3.25"

$15-18.

Rare. $45-50.

$10-12.

Experimental, not priced.

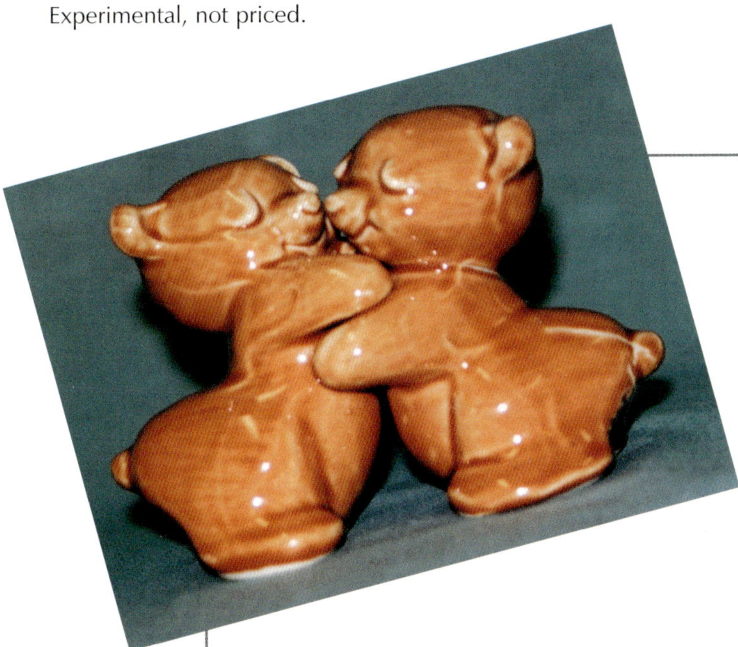

$8-10.

Bendel Bears. 4". $55-65.

Van Tellingen Ducks.
3.75". $35-40.

Van Tellingen Ducks.
3.75". $25-30.

Van Tellingen Bunnies. 3.75"

$15-18.

Label, "Hand Painted, Stieff Art Studio, Linthicum Post Office, Maryland." $25-30.

$25-30.

$20-25

Van Tellingen Bunnies. 3.75"

$18-20.

$25-30.

$18-20.

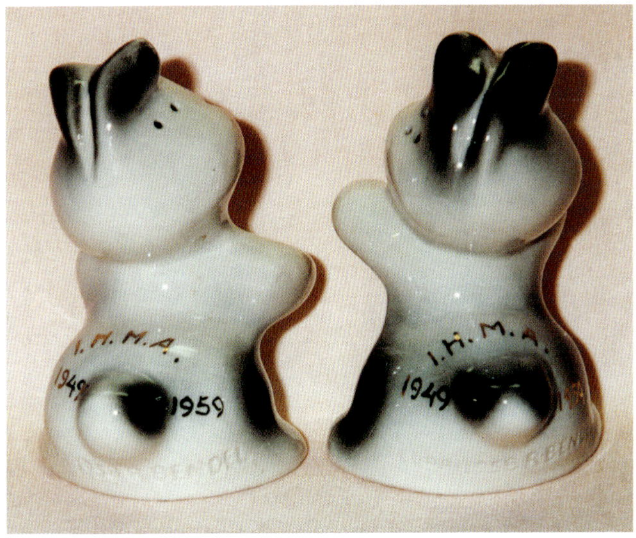

Bendel Bunnies. 4". $125-135. Side and back views.

Bendel Love Bugs. 3.5". $60-65. Shows color variations.

Bendel Love Bugs

Rare. 3.5". $90-100.

3.5". $60-65.

3.5". Experimental, not priced.

Very rare. 3.5". $600+.

4.25". $90-100.

Van Tellingen pigs. 4". $350+.

Bendel pigs. 6.75". $275-300. Together and apart.

Van Tellingen pigs. 4.5". $450+.

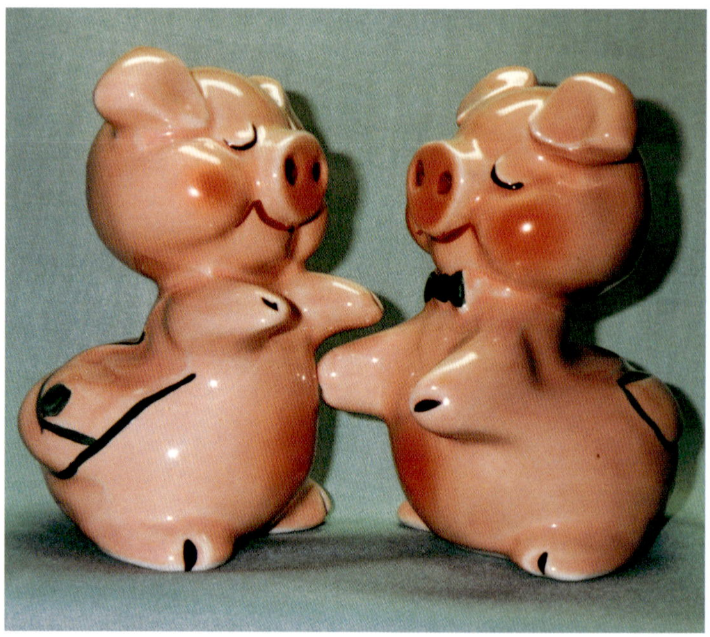

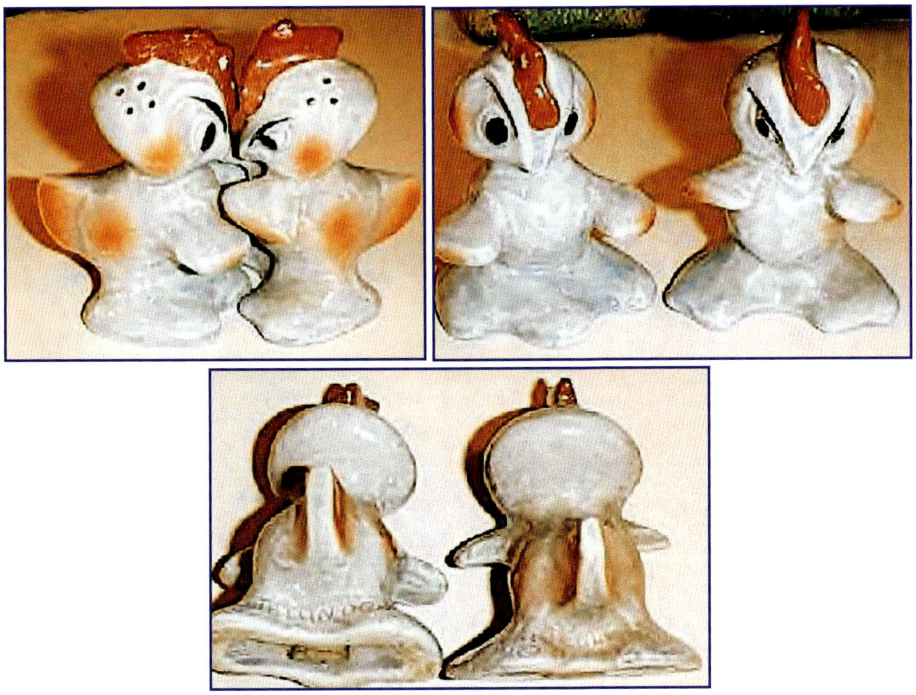

Van Tellingen roosters. 3.75". Sold at auction in 2001 for $1500.

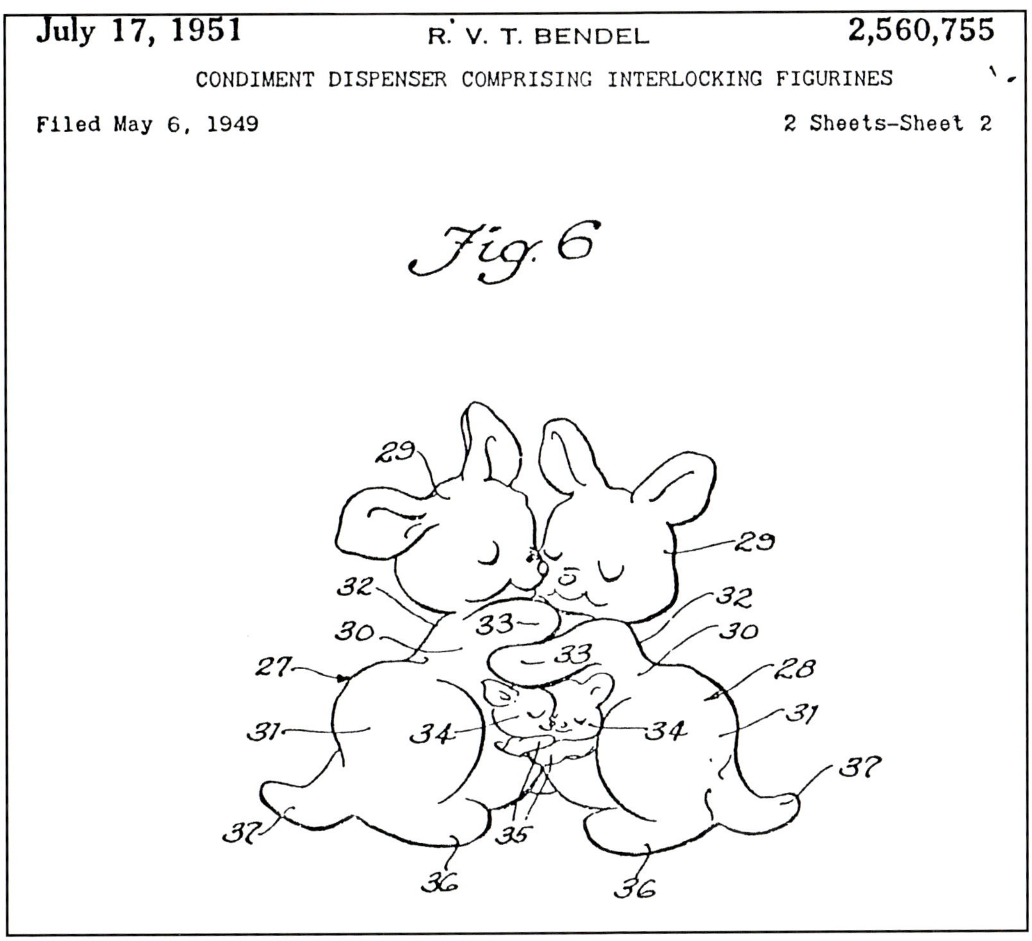

Snuggle Hugs Kangaroo patent application drawing. Although the application was filed, no sets have been found to date.

Van Tellingen Boy and Dog. 3.5".

$45-50.

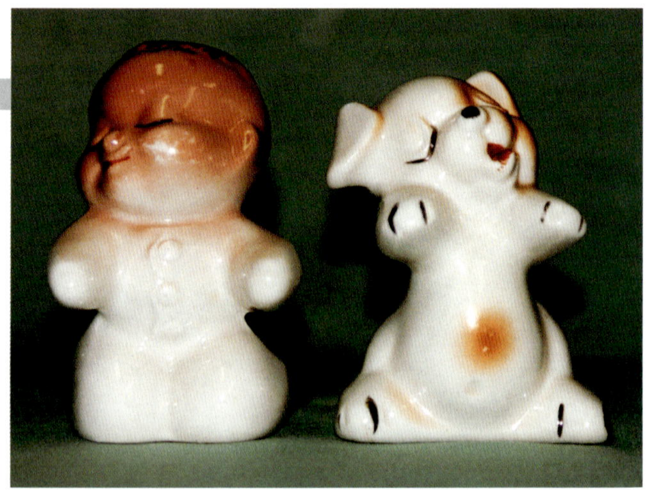

$40-45.

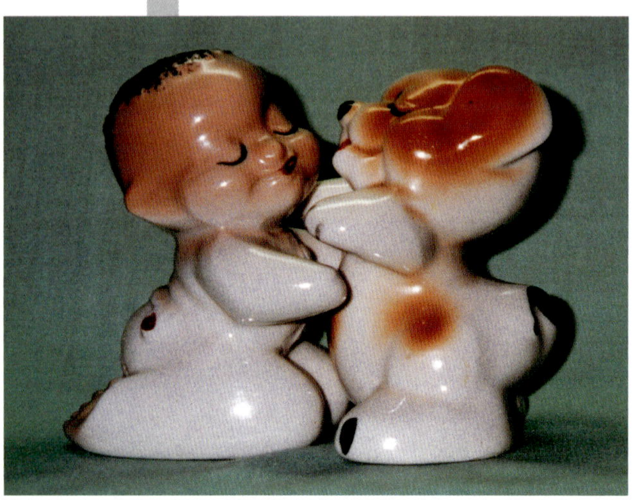

$35-40.

Van Tellingen Dutch Boy and Girl. 3.75". $25-30. Together, apart, and without accent color.

Van Tellingen Sailor and Mermaid. 4". $95-100.

Van Tellingen Mary and her Lamb. 3.75". $35-40.

Experimental, not priced.

Chickens. 5". $75-85.

FiFi. 5". Made for Jim Beam Club members and personalized if requested. $125-150.

Cats. 4.25". $75-85.

Blossom Valley Foxes. $110-125.

The fox is the mascot of the Jim Beam International Association. Five hundred of these sets were made as gifts to convention attendees at the Jim Beam Bottle Club convention in San Jose, California.

5.75". Front and back views.

5.75".

4.5". Males, two and three holes.

Dutch girl. 4.75". $150-175.

C. Miller clowns. 4.25". $150-175.

French chefs. 4.25". $150-175.

French chefs, not Regal China.

Alice in Wonderland. 5". $225-250. Incised © Walt Disney Productions.

Alice in Wonderland. 5". $350-375.

Goldilocks. 4.5". $200-225.

Goldilocks. 4.5". $150-175.

Goldilocks, not Regal China.

Tweedle Dee and Tweedle Dum. 4.5". $800+.

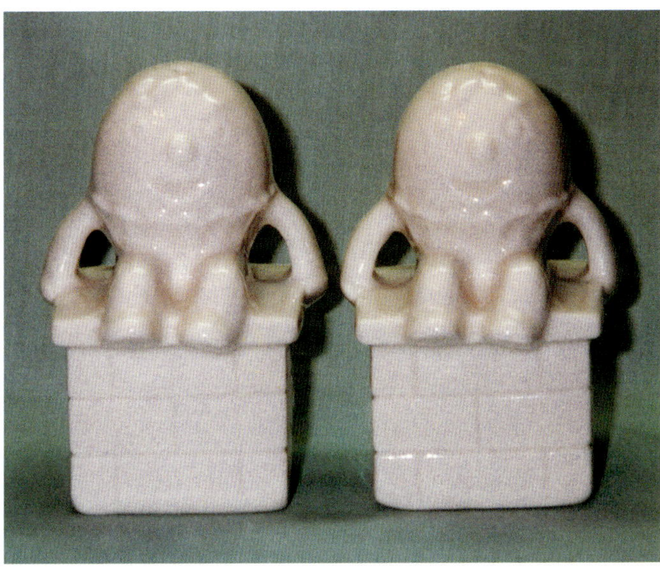

Humpty Dumpty. 4.25". $75-85.

Peek-a-Boos. 3.5".

$150-175.

$175-200.

$225-250.

Peek-a-Boos. 5". $300-325.

Peek-a-Boos. 5". $375-400.

Tulips. 4.5". $18-20. Front and back views.

Peek-a-Boos. 5". $325-350.

C. Miller pigs. 4". $25-35. One piece.

C. Miller pigs. 4". $45-50. One piece.

C. Miller fish. 3.75". $45-50. One piece.

C. Miller fish. 3.75". $25-35. One piece.

Old MacDonald's Farm. These sets were produced as part of a kitchenware group that included a canister set, cookie jar, creamer/sugar, teapots, greaser, and butter dish.

Butter churns. 3.75". $55-65.

Butter churns. 3.75". $35-45.

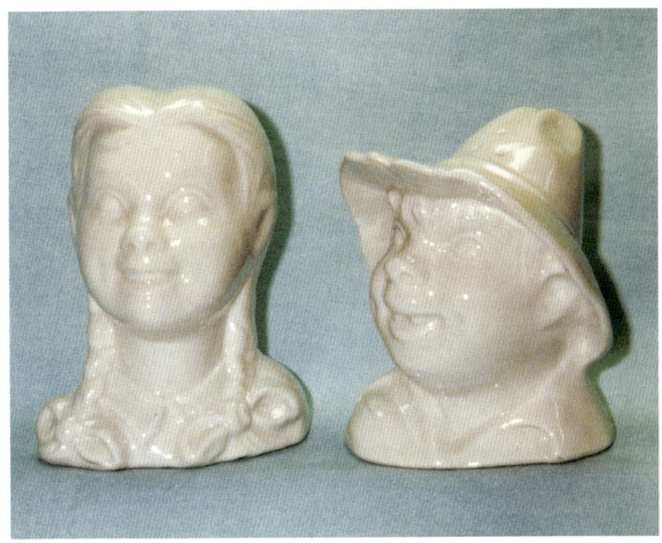

Farmer boy and girl. 4". $45-50.

Feed sacks. 5".
$100-125 pair.

Feed sacks. 5".
$85-90.

Convention Sets

"A Nod to Abe." 5.5". Special trim number one 1991 Club convention set. This set was designed by Betty Harrington, the primary designer for Ceramic Arts Studio, Madison, Wisconsin. Four hundred sets were produced by Regal China Co. This set sold at the convention auction for $1100.

"A Nod to Abe." 5.5". Issue price $35. 1991 Club convention set available to Club members. $225-250.

"Leaf People." 3.75". 1992 Club convention set. $175-200.

Little Red Riding Hood.

These sets were designed by the Hull Pottery Company of Ohio and produced by Regal China from 1943 to 1957. Shown are the three sizes, matching sets, and several shakers with trim variations.

3.25". $65-75.

3.25". $65-75.

3.25". $400+.

Little Red Riding Hood.
4.5". $600+.

Little Red Riding Hood.
5.25". $100-125.

Blue Ridge

Blue Ridge dinnerware was produced by Southern Potteries of Erwin, Tennessee from the late 1930s until 1956. Several color variations are found in the figural chicken sets.

Chickens. 4.5". $100-125.

Ducks. 4". $200-225.

Elbee Art

Elbee Art Company was established in Cleveland, Ohio in 1941. No further information was found. These sets have a high gloss finish.

Alligators. 3". $8-10.

Bears. 4". $10-12.

Monkey. 3.75". $10-12.

Cats. 2.75". $10-12.

Horse heads. 2.5". $8-10.

Dog and phonograph. 3.5". $12-15.
Also found as two phonographs.

Elephants. 3". $12-15 with gold, $10-12 without.

Elephant. 4.25".
$10-12.

Rabbits. 5.5".
$12-15.

Skunks. 3.75".
$10-12.

Pigs. 2.75 - 3". $10-12.

Birds on branches.
2.75 - 4". $12-15.

Birds. 2.75". $6-8.

Chickens. 3". $8-10.

Chicks. 2". $8-10.

Chickens. 2.5". $8-10.

Chickens. 4.5". $10-12.

Chickens. 2". $8-10.

Chickens. 2.5". $8-10.

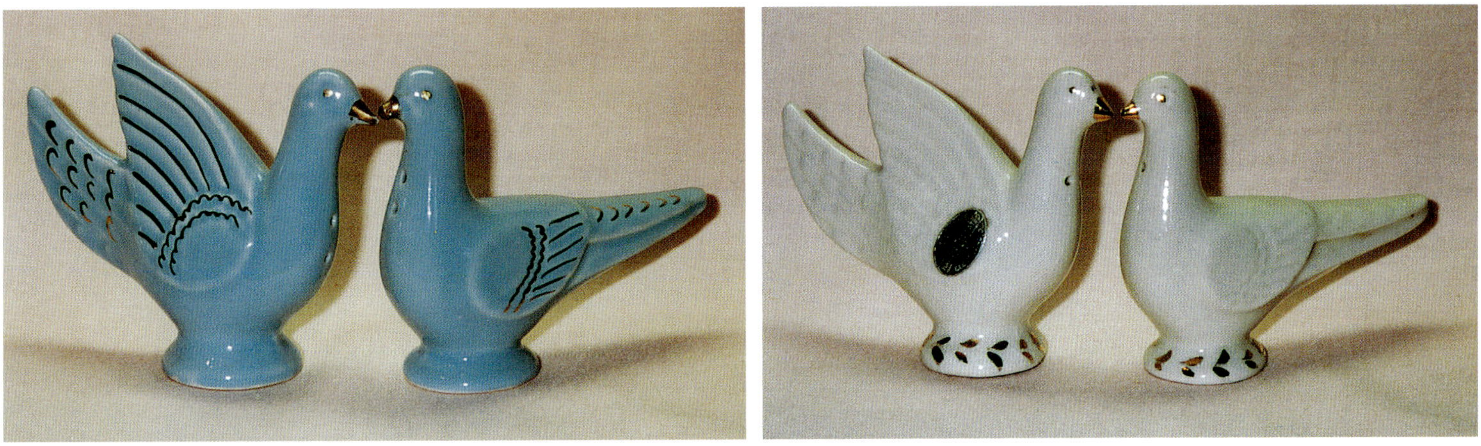

Doves. 3.25". $8-10.

Owls. 2". $6-8.

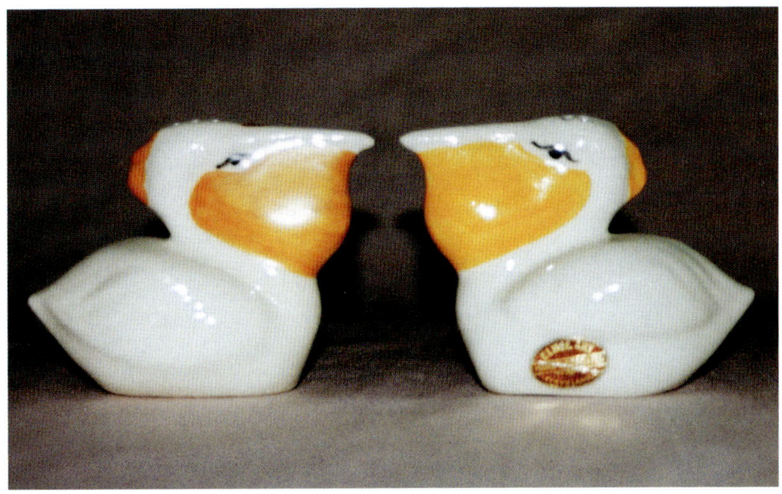

Pelicans. 3". $8-10.

Ducks. 4.25". $10-12.

Pheasants. 2.75". $10-12.

Fish. 2.75". $10-12.

Flamingos. 3.75". $12-15.

Frog and mushroom. 3". $8-10.

Seals. 4.5". $10-12.

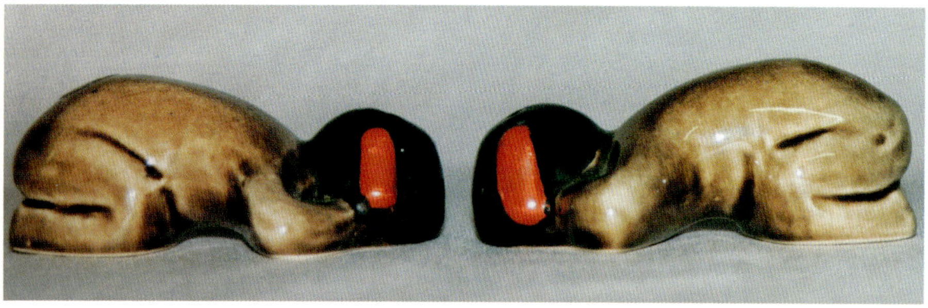

"Hi Nosey," incised. 1.5". $35-40.

Clowns. 3.75". $18-20.

Clowns. 4.25". $20-25.

Elves. 3". $10-12.

Pilgrims. 4". $12-15.

Devil and angel. 4". $12-15.

Fishermen. 2.25". $12-15.

Santa Claus. 4". $12-15.

Santa Claus and Christmas tree. 4". $15-18.

Cowboy and cowgirl. 3.75". $15-18.

Musicians. 4". $18-20.

Hockey player. 3.75". $18-20.

Mexican couple. 4". $15-18.

Square dancers. 4.25". $18-20. Two views.

Native Americans. 3.5". $15-18.

Oriental couples.
3.25-4". $15-18.

Dutch boy and windmill. 3.5". $12-15.

Dutch girl and windmill. 3.5". $12-15.

Dutch couple. 2.75". $12-15.

Dutch couple. 4". $12-15.

Oriental couple. 4.5". $12-15.

Mexican couple. 3.5". $12-15.

Ladies. 3.25". $15-18. With gold, $18-20. Black ladies, $25-30.

Baseball and glove.
1.5". $8-10.

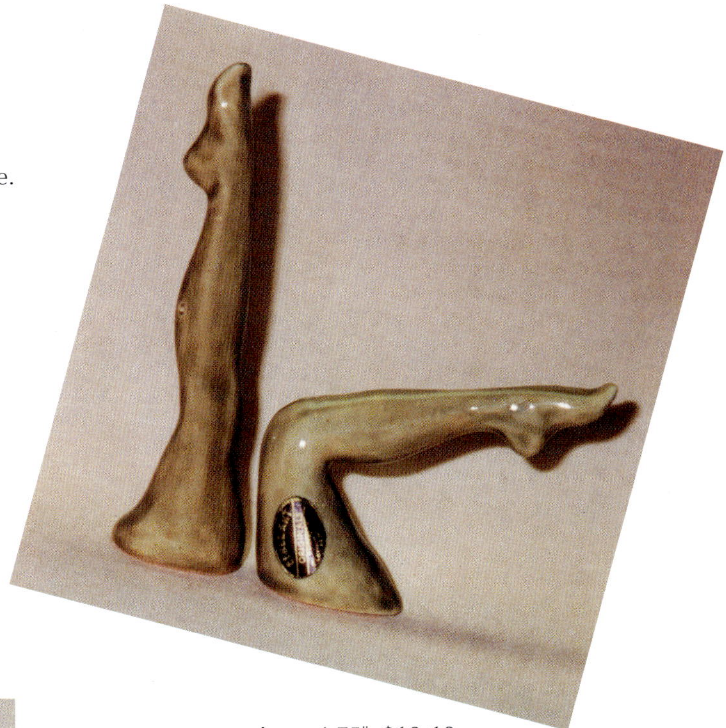

Legs. 4.75". $10-12.

Corn with husks on tray.
1.5". $10-12.

Bookworm and book.
2.5". $12-15.

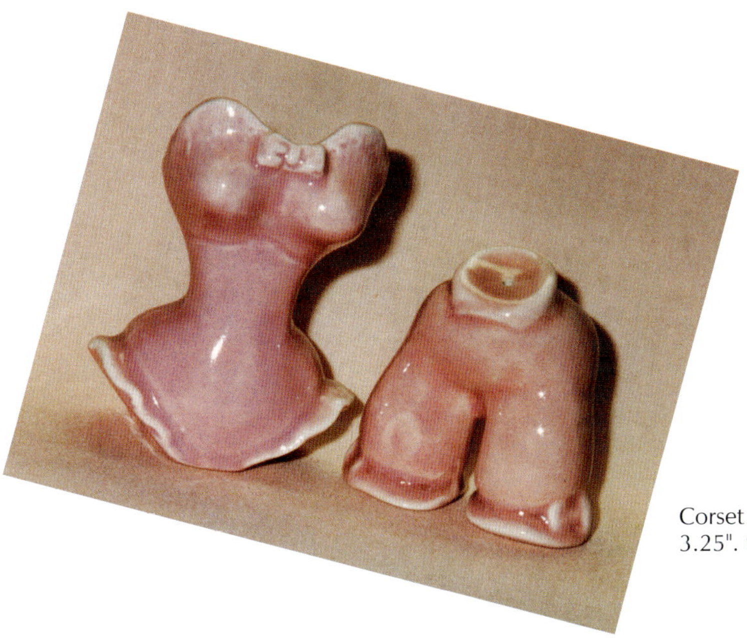

Corset and bloomers.
3.25". $10-12.

Flowers. 2". $8-10.

Roses. 1.75". $8-10.

Calla lilies. 2.25". $8-10.

Poppies. 2.5". $6-8.

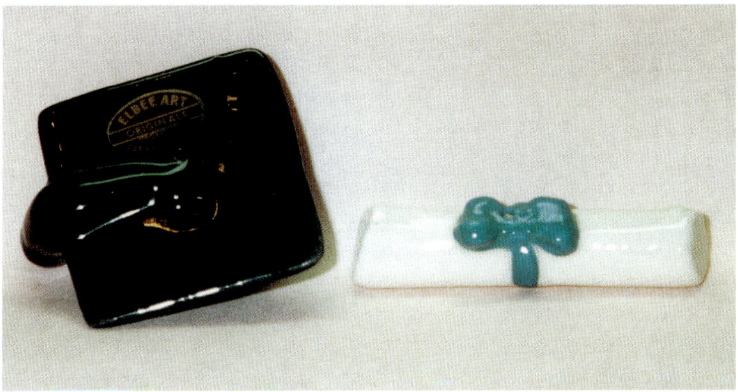

Graduation hat and diploma. 1". $8-10.

Houses in holder. 2.25". $8-10.

Phonographs. 3.25". $6-8.

Lamps. 3.5". $8-10.

Telephones. 2.5". $6-8.

Totem poles. 3.5". $8-10.

Seltzer bottles. 4.25". $8-10.

Trains. 2.25". $25-30 for complete train of two sets.

Vases. 4.25". $6-8.

Windmills. 3.5". $8-10.

California Potteries

Barnware

These sets were made by Vera LaFountain Dunn of Hollywood, California in the mid 1940s. The label says "An original Barnware design, Vera LaFountain Dunn, Hollywood, California," as shown below.

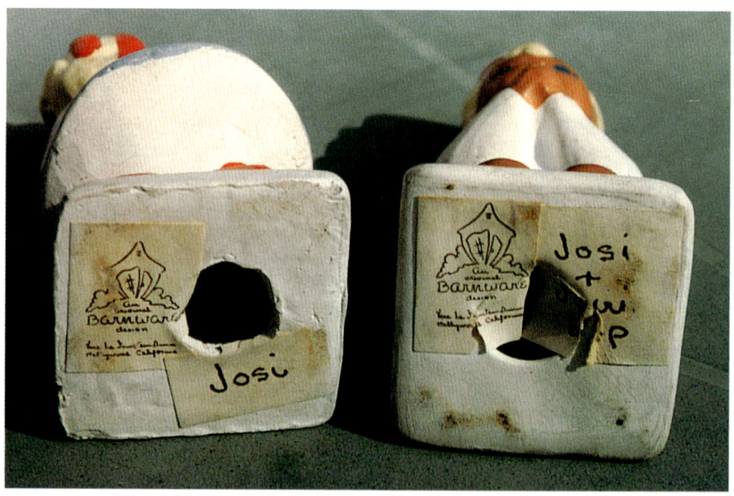

Recently located information shows a label marked "barnware, created by verdan lolayne, california, u.s.a. copyright." We are uncertain as to whether the labels represent one or two pottery artists. The products look very similar.

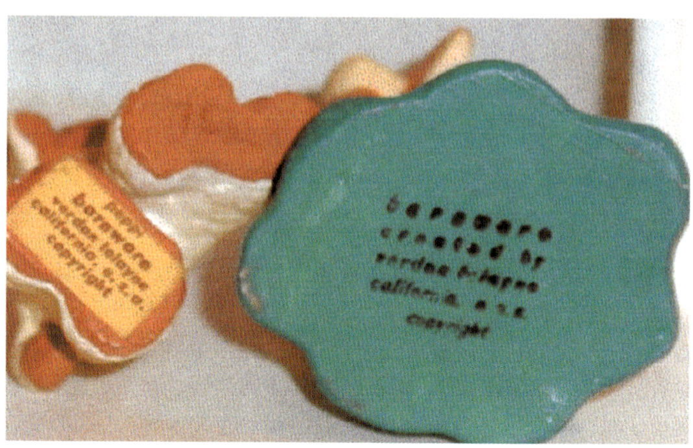

Josi and Joni. 3.75". $30-35.

Lezginka single. 6". $30-35 pair.

Flack and Frohna. 3.75". $30-35.

Girls. 3.75". $30-35.

Boy and girl. 3.75". $30-35.

Sascha Brastoff

From 1947 to 1963, Sascha Brastoff headed a ceramics business in Los Angeles. Using new and unusual materials, a flamboyant style of decoration, and substantial gold trim, he produced unique designs. While all pieces made were signed, only those with a full name were personally crafted by Brastoff; the others were usually produced under his supervision. Although his salt and peppers are beautiful, we have seen few figural ones to date.

Huskies. 4". $55-65.

Seal and shaker without picture. 5.5". $75-85.
Blank shaker probably a manufacturing error.

Seals. 4". $45-55.

Bighorn sheep. 4". $55-65.

Walrus. 4". $45-55.

Eskimos. 4". $45-55.

Igloos. 4". $35-45.

Igloos. 4". $35-45.

Icebergs. 4". $35-45.

Food caches. 4". $35-45.

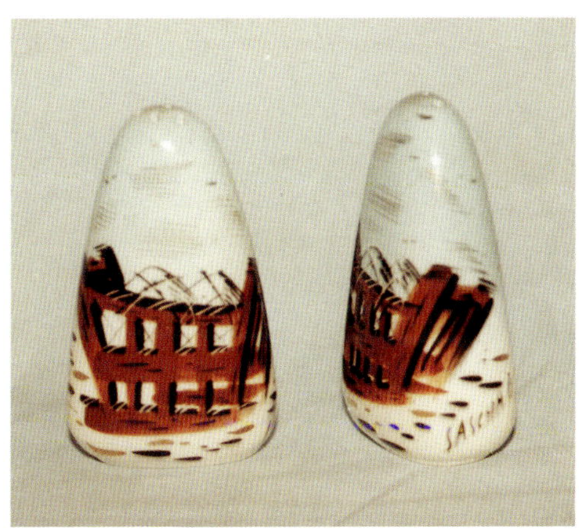

Dog sleds. 4". $35-45.

Dinnerware Patterns

Right & Far right: Smoke Tree. 4". $25-30.

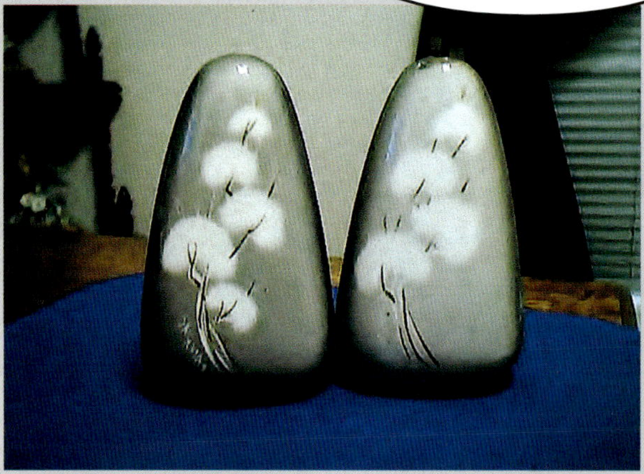

Leaf. 4". $20-25.

Tulip. 4". $20-25.

Surf Ballet. 4". $25-30.

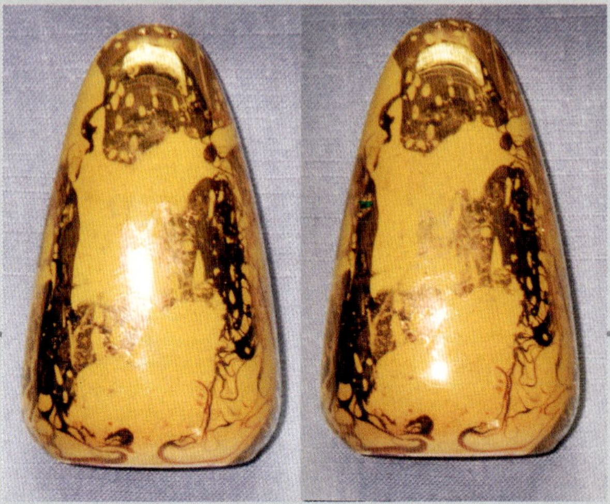

Pepper Mill Mechanisms.

Contributor Verity Hobbs provided some interesting information. She moved with her family from England to California in 1948. Her father established a factory in Altadena, subsequently moved to Laguna Beach, to make pepper mill mechanisms and assemble the pepper mills. He named the factory Verity Southall Ltd., combining her name with the name of the English town where his first factory was located. Grinders made of Sheffield steel were imported from England and assembled into the pepper mills. Mechanisms are marked Verity Southall Ltd. Customers for these products included Sascha Brastoff, Vernon Kilns, Gladding-McBean, and other potteries. The factory was sold in 1970 to an El Segundo company. All sets 7". $125-150 pair.

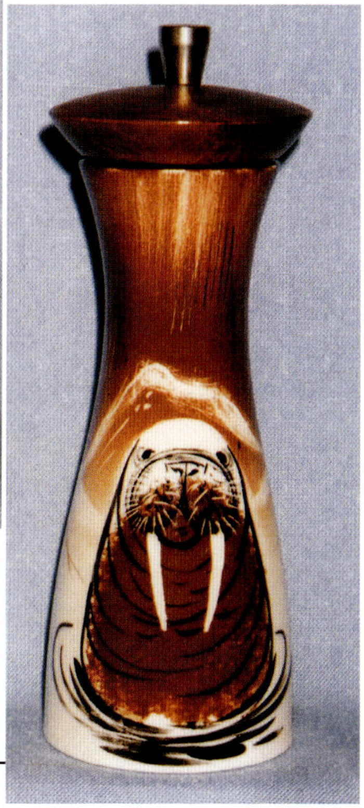

Walrus.

Seals.

Husky single.

Igloos.

Eskimos.

Oriental design.

Matthew Adams

Matthew Adams worked with Sascha Brastoff in the early 1950s, where he produced the "Alaska" ceramic line, created for a gift shop in Anchorage. After leaving Brastoff's company, he continued to design and produce Alaska pottery in California. His pieces are signed Matthew or Matt Adams as shown below. A black "Alaska" logo was added at the request of the Ketchikan Trading Post; this was changed to gold in the 1980s. Adams continued to produce items until his retirement in 1998.

Kodiak bears. 5.25". $100-110.

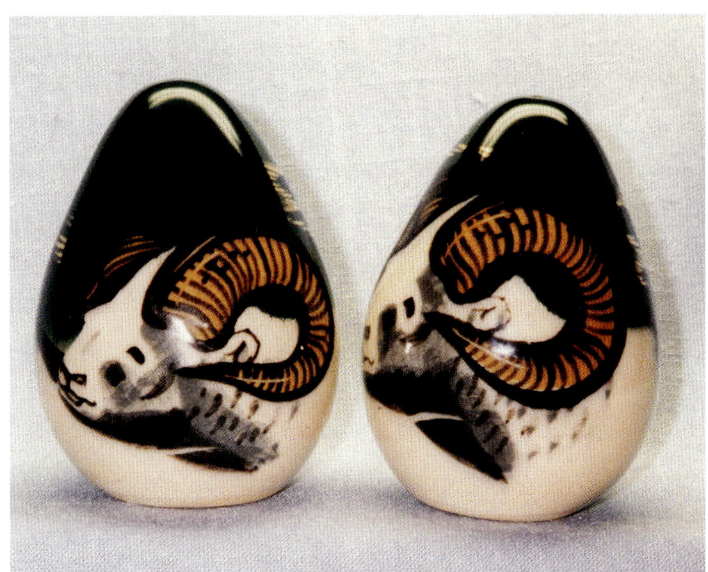

Bighorn sheep. 3.75". $75-85.

Polar Bear heads.
3.75". $65-75.

Polar Bear heads. 3.75". $65-75.

Polar Bear heads. 5.25". $90-100.

Polar Bear Heads.
5.25". $90-100.

Standing Polar Bears.
3.75". $65-75.

Standing Polar Bears.
5.25". $90-100.

Moose. 3.75". $75-85.

Seals. 3.75". $65-75.

Seals. 3.75". $65-75.

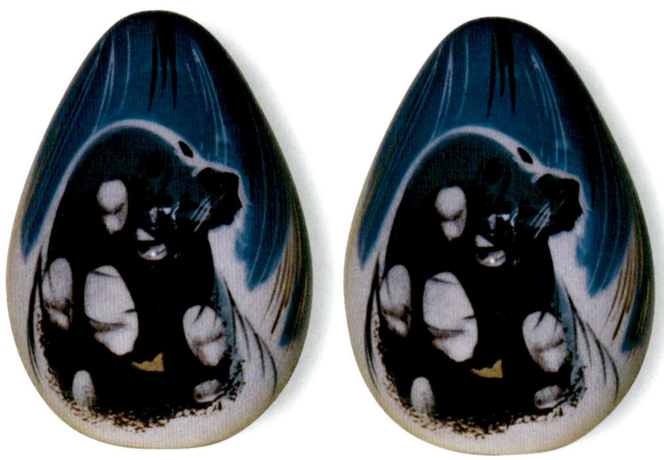

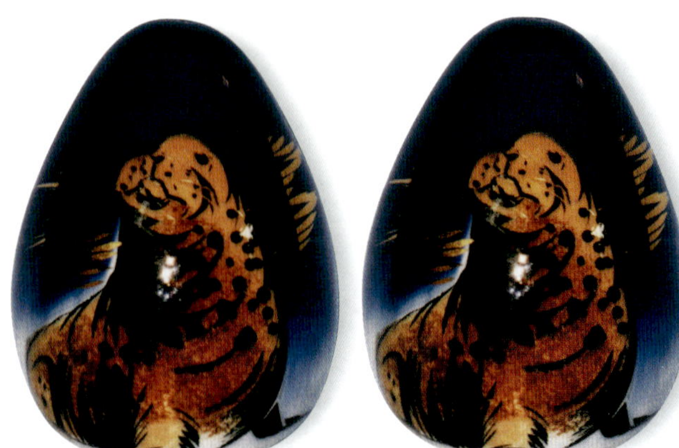

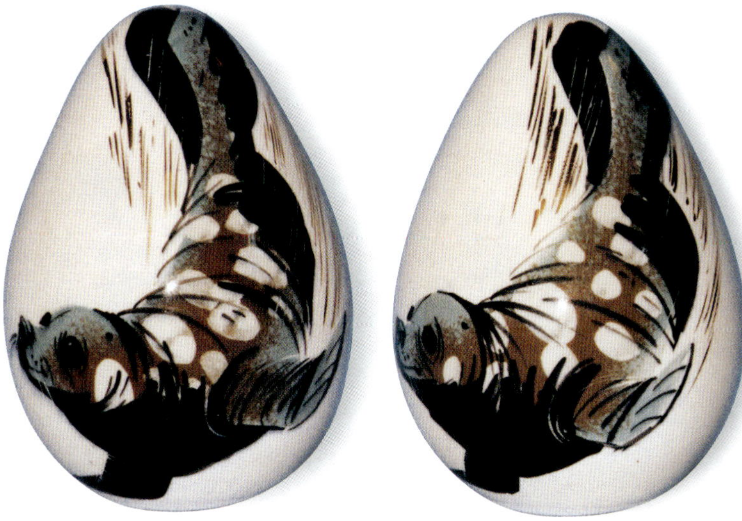

Seals. 5.25". $90-100.

Walrus. 5.25". $90-100.

Walrus. 3.75". $65-75.

Eskimos. 3.75". $65-75.

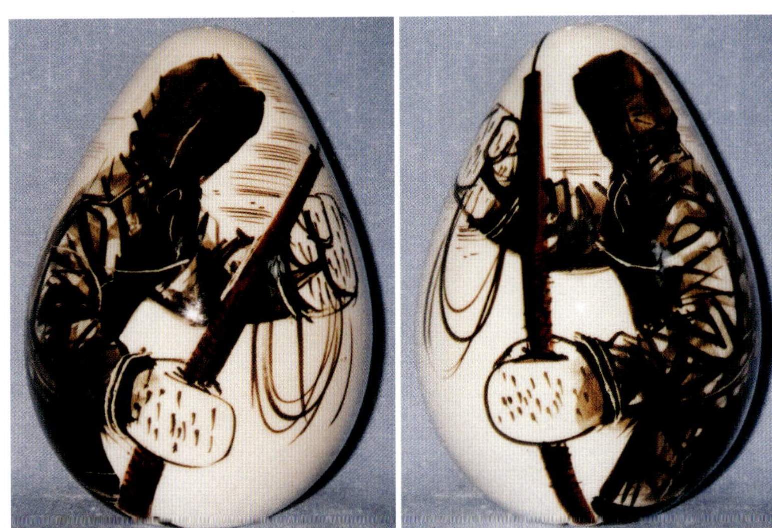

Eskimo with harpoon. 5.25". $100-110.

Eskimos. 5.25". $90-100.

Igloos. 5.25". $70-80.

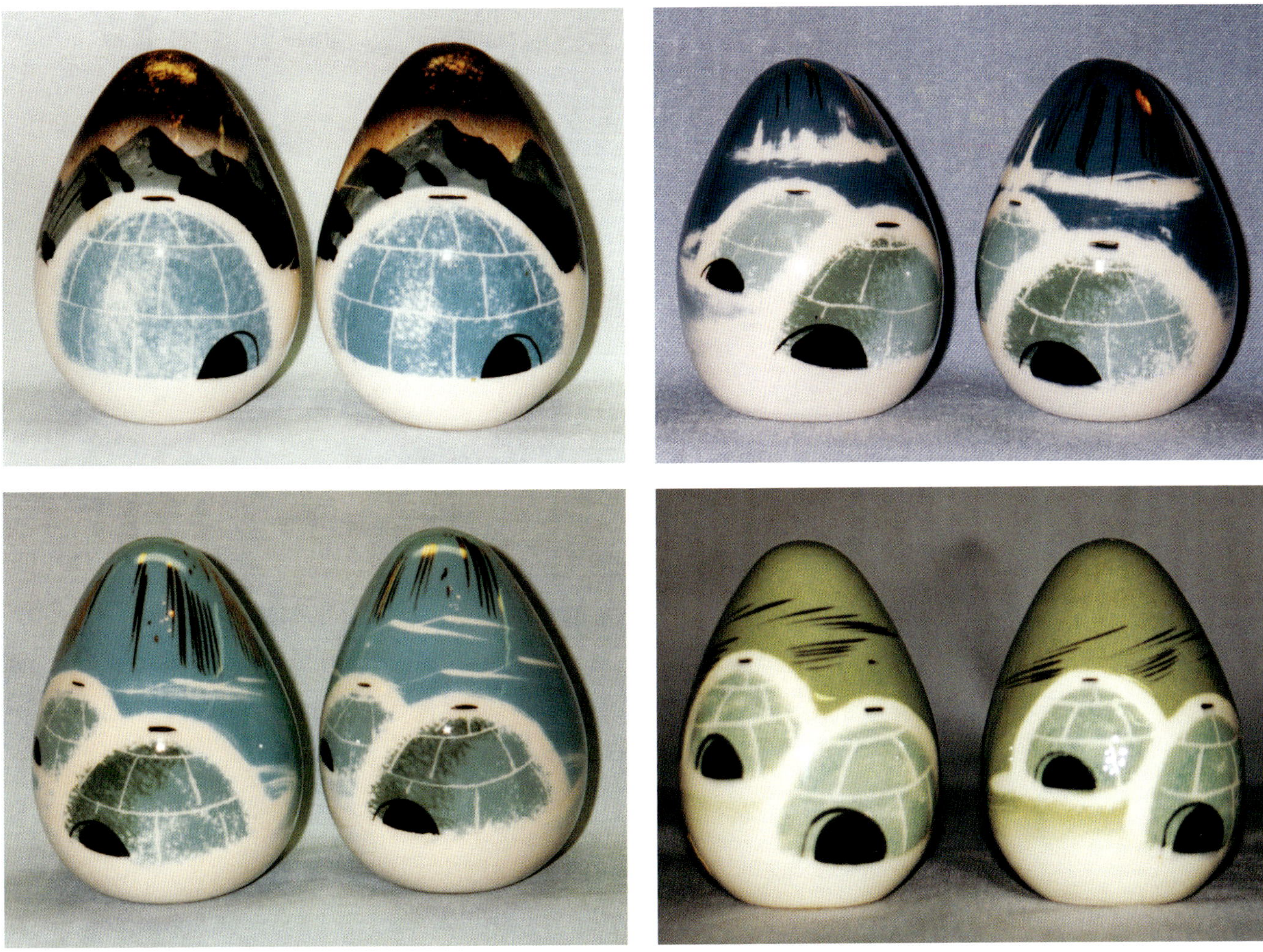

Igloos. 3.75". $45-55.

Igloos. 5.25". $70-80.

Icebergs. 3.75". $45-55.

Sled and igloo. 3.75". $60-70.

Food caches. 3.75". $45-55.

Food caches. 5.25". $70-80.

Catalina

Catalina Island Pottery, made on the island of the same name located off the coast of Southern California, was started in 1927. The business was conceived by chewing gum tycoon William Wrigley, Jr., owner of the island, and an associate. Local brown clay and pulverized rock were used in the manufacturing process. Glazes were developed using native oxides. The combination of these glazes and the clay provided distinctive pottery. The company was sold to Gladding-McBean in 1937 and became known as Catalina Pottery.

Penguins. 4". $85-95.

Mexican couple. 4". $150-175.

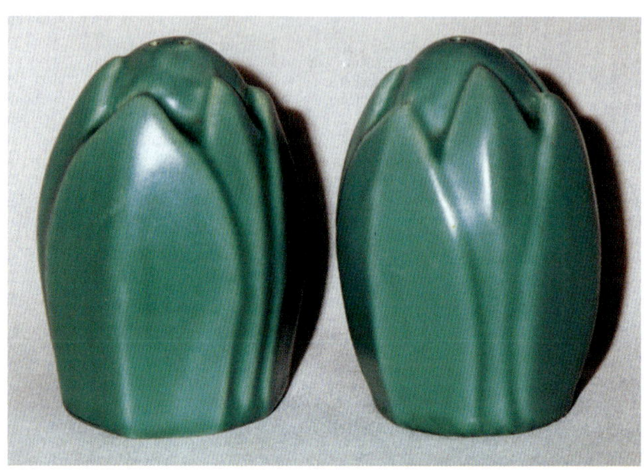

Tulips. 3". $65-75.

The California Cleminsons

This pottery began in 1941 as a hobby of Betty Cleminson and was initially housed in a garage in Monterey Park, California. In 1943, a factory was constructed in El Monte. One very successful product was a tableware line called Distelfink, featuring a bird motif in Pennsylvania Dutch style. The pottery closed in 1963.

Distelfink birds. 4.75". $25-30.

Artists. 6". $45-50.

Kangaroo. 6". $35-40.

"Galagray." 6.75". $35-40. Two views.

Sailors. 5.25". $35-40. Front and back views.

Hearts on stand. 2.5". $25-30.

Packages. 1.5". $20-25.

Franciscan Ware

The Franciscan plant of Gladding-McBean was California's largest pottery. The company was founded in 1875. Initial Franciscan pattern production began in 1937, followed by the Apple pattern in 1940, Desert Rose in 1942, and Ivy in 1948. The plant was sold to another company in 1962 and then to Wedgwood and Sons, Ltd. of England in 1979. Wedgwood continues to manufacture some of these items.

Desert Rose and Cafe Royale. 2.5". $15-18.

Apple. 2.25". $15-18.

California Poppy. 3". $30-35.

Ivy. 3". $25-30.

Gibson California Arts

No information has been located on this pottery. Sets found bear a diamond shaped label.

Cats. 4.5 - 5.25". $10-12.

Pekingese. 3.5". $10-12.

Horses. 3". $10-12.

Elephants. 3". $10-12.

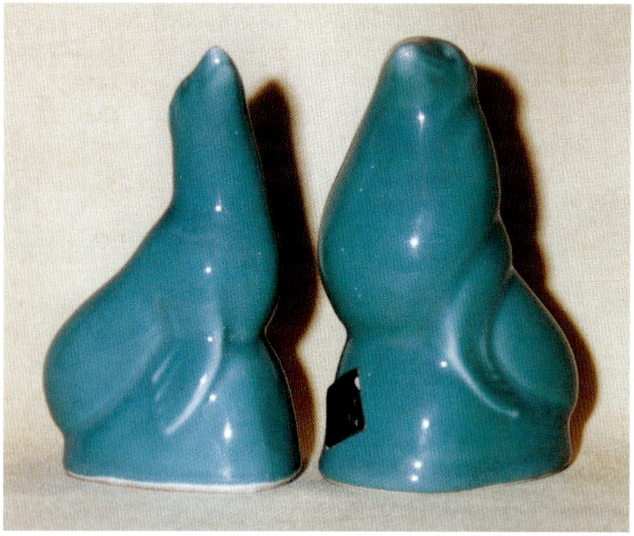

Seals. 3.5". $10-12.

Elves. 2.75". $10-12.

Pear and apple. 3.25". $10-12.

Apples. 2". $5-8.

Artichoke.
3.25". $6-8.

Oriental couple. 3.25". $10-12.

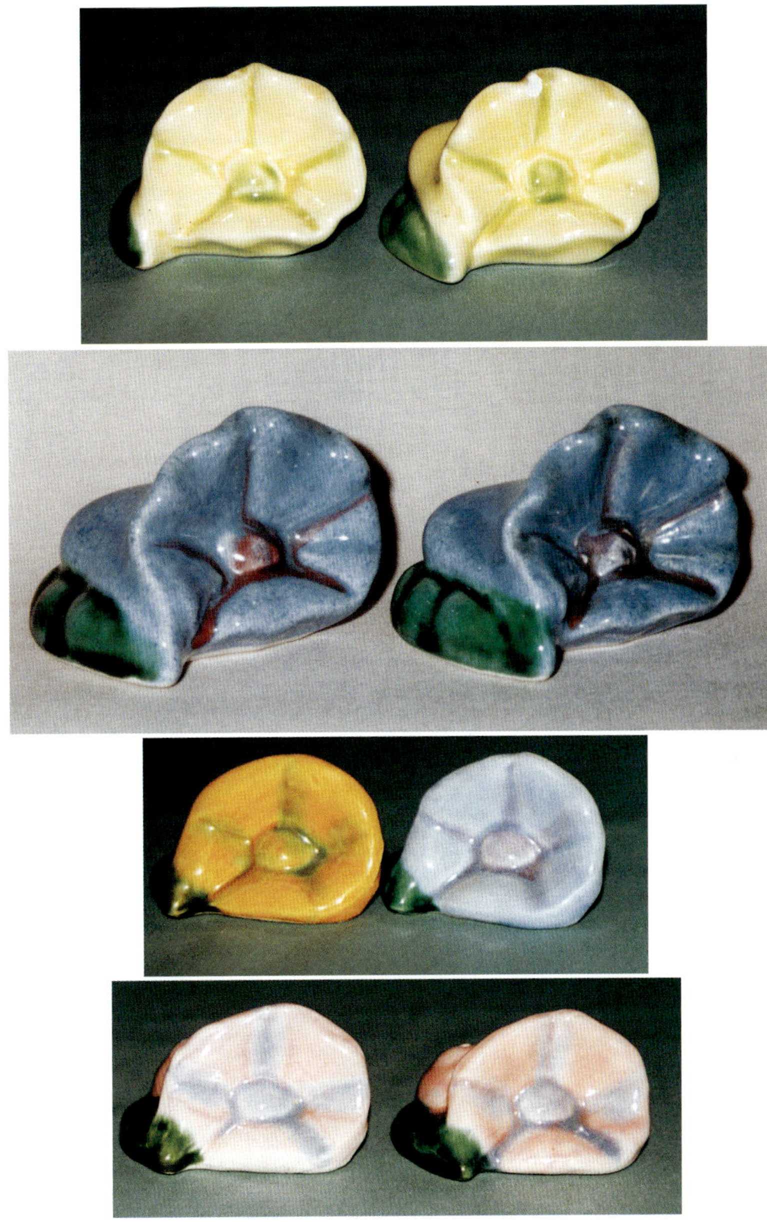

Morning glories. 2.25". $6-8.

Calla lilies. 2.5". $6-8.

Roselane

Roselane Pottery was started in 1938 by William and Georgia Fields. Initially located in their California home, production was moved to Pasadena in 1940 and then to Baldwin Park. Principal lines were the Sparkler series, Aqua Marine, and Chinese Modern. The pottery closed in the mid-1970s.

Aqua Marine pattern. 5.5". $30-35.

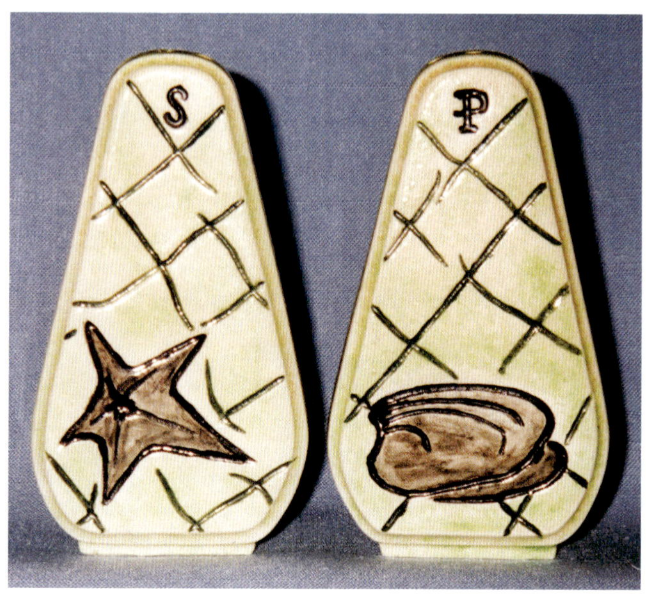

Lobster pattern. 5". $18-20. Front and back views.

Margaret Weese

Margaret Weese and Billee Vier were pottery artists in the late 1940s and early 1950s in Manhattan Beach, California. They sold their original designs at local markets. Weese shakers are marked with either the initials MW or the name MWeese, as shown below.

Animals, Etc.

Bees. 2.25". $10-12.

Bird and house. 2.5". $12-15.

Bison. 3". $12-15.

Butterflies. 2.5". $12-15.

Cats. 2.5 - 2.75". $12-15.

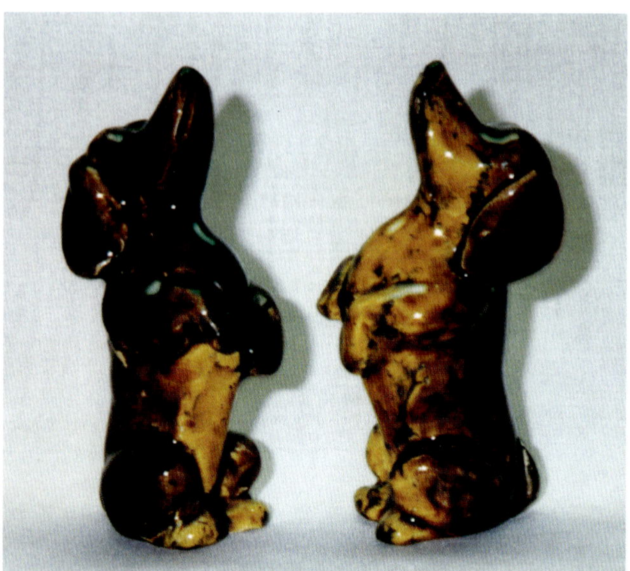

Dachshunds. 3.5". $15-18.

Ducks. 2.75". $12-15.

Fish. 1.25". Single. $10-12 pair.

Elephant. 4". Single. $12-15 pair.

Elephant and drum. 3.25". $12-15.

Hippopotamus and rhinoceros. 2.25". $15-18.

Dragons. 2.25". $15-18.

Goat and can. 3.75". $18-20.

Dragons. 2.75". $10-20.

Frogs. 1.75". $12-15.

Lions. 4". $18-20.

Mouse and cheese. 1.75". $12-15.

Royal mice. 2". $15-18.

Parrots. 2.75". $15-18.

Ostriches. 4.5". $18-20.

Rabbit. 5.25". Single. $15-18 pair.

Owls. 3". $15-18.

Rabbits. 3". $12-15.

Peacocks. 2.5". $18-20.

Seal with ball. 2.25". $18-20.

Squirrels. 1.75". $12-15.

Turtles. 1". $10-12.

Tigers. 3". $18-20.

Alice in Wonderland and White Rabbit. 3.25". $35-40.

Cheshire Cat and Caterpillar. 4". $35-40.

Tweedle Dee and Tweedle Dum. 3". $35-40.

Mad Hatters. 4.25". $35-40.

King and Queen of Hearts. 3.5". $30-35.

Cupid. 2.25". $25-30.

Father Time. 3.75". $25-30.

Humpty Dumpty. 3". $25-30. Stacker.

Gingerbread men. 1.25". $20-25.

Daniel Boone and beaver. 3.5". $25-30.

Paul Bunyan and Babe. 3.25". $25-30.

Little Bo Peep. 1.75". $20-25.

Little Miss Muffet and Little Bo Peep. 3". $25-30.

Knight and dragon. 4.25". $35-40.

Peter, Peter Pumpkin Eater and wife. 3.5". $25-30.

Mary and her Lamb. 3". $25-30.

Laurel and Hardy. 4". $25-30.

Pan. 3.25". $20-25.

Sing a Song of Sixpence. 4". $25-30.

Jack Spratt and wife. 4". $25-30.

Mr. and Mrs. Potato Head. 2.25 - 2.75". $20-25.

Pinocchio. 4.25". $20-25.

Uncle Sam and world. 4". $35-40.

George and Martha Washington. 3.5". $30-35.

George and Martha Washington. 3.5". $40-45.

George Washington and tree stump. 4". $30-35.

Carousel. 3". $18-20.

Clowns. 4". Two singles. $18-20 pair.

Clowns. 4". $18-20.

Clown. 3.5". $18-20. Stacker.

Clowns. 3.5". $18-20.

Magician and rabbit. 3.5". $15-18.

Gypsy and monkey. 3". $12-15.

Fat Lady. 2.5". Single.
$15-18 pair.

Bearded Lady and Snake Charmer. 3". $35-40.

Animal tamer. 4". Possibly singles. $12-15 pair.

Lion tamer. 3.5". Possibly singles. $12-15 pair.

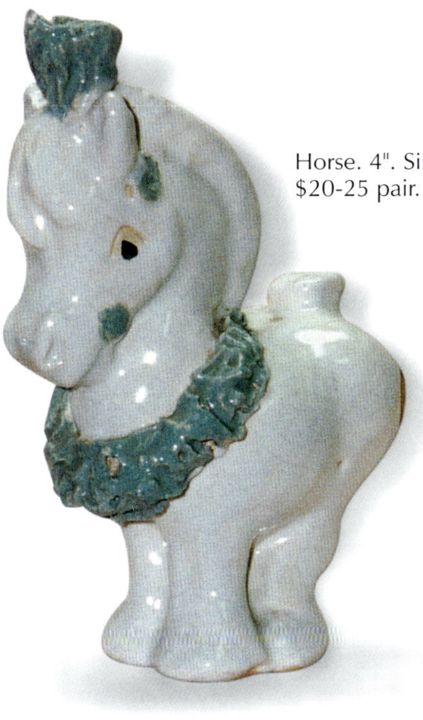

Horse. 4". Single.
$20-25 pair.

Ringmaster and horse. 4.25". $20-25.

Holidays

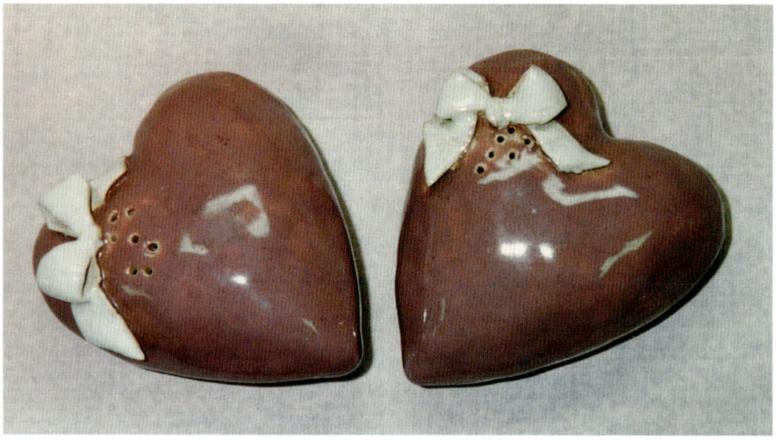

Valentine hearts. 1.5". $12-15.

Easter eggs. 2". $12-15.

Scarecrow and tombstone. 3.25". $15-18.

Witch and crow. 3.25". $15-18.

Ghost and shock of corn. 3.25". $15-18.

Pilgrim and turkey. 4.75". $30-35. Front and back views.

Pilgrim lady. 3". Single. $15-18 pair.

Pilgrim couple. 3". $15-18.

Pilgrim and Indian. 3.25". $20-25.

Christmas angels. 3". $18-20.

Angels and Devils

Angels. 2". $12-15.

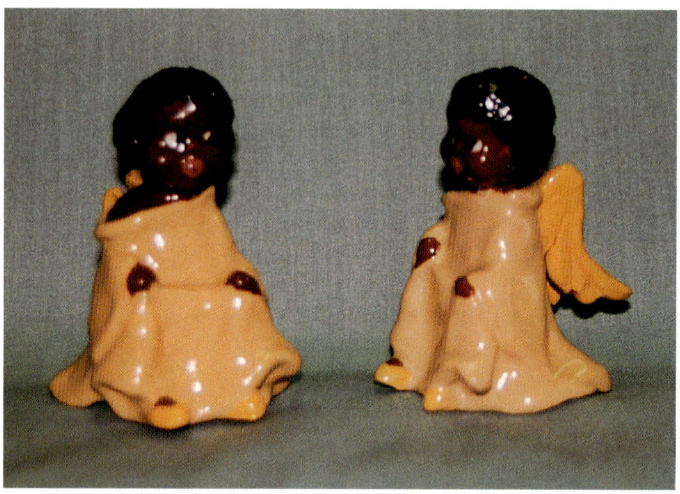

Angels. 3". $20-25.

Cherubs. 1.75". $10-12.

Devils. 3". $10-12.

People in Uniform

Sailors. 3 - 4". $12-15 pair.

Russian sailors. 2.5". $12-15.

Scout leader and scout. 3.75". $15-18.

Scout leaders. 3.75". $15-18.

Musical

Choir singers. 2.5 - 3". $12-15.

Ballet dancers. 3.5". $12-15.

Barbershop quartet. 4". $25-30 complete group of two sets.

Square dancers. 3.75". $12-15.

Square dancer. 3". Single. $12-15 pair.

Square dancers. 4". $15-18. One set incised 3/21/50.

Russian dancers. 4". $20-25.

Mummers. 3.5". $35-40.

Girl playing piano. 1.75 - 2.25". $12-15.

Girl playing piano. 2.5". $15-18.

Band members. 4.25". $18-20.

Mexican couple. 3.5". $18-20

Occupations

Artist and model. 4". $18-20.

Bellhops. 2.75". $20-25. "Call for Philip Morris."

Cowboy and horse. 4". $12-15.

Cowboy and donkey. 3.75". $12-15.

Dentist and patient. 3". $18-20.

Cook. 2.75". Single.
$10-12 pair.

Farmer and cow. 4.5". $12-15.

Firemen. 3.5". $12-15.

Deep sea diver and mermaid. 3.5". $20-25.

Mail carriers. 3". Single. $15-18 pair.

Fisherman and wife. 3". $18-20.

Policemen. 3.5". $15-18.

Pirate and chest. 3.75". $18-20.

King and Queen. 4.5". $20-25.

Queen and page. 4.5". $20-25.

Waitresses. 2.5". $15-18.

Railroad conductors. 3.25". $15-18.

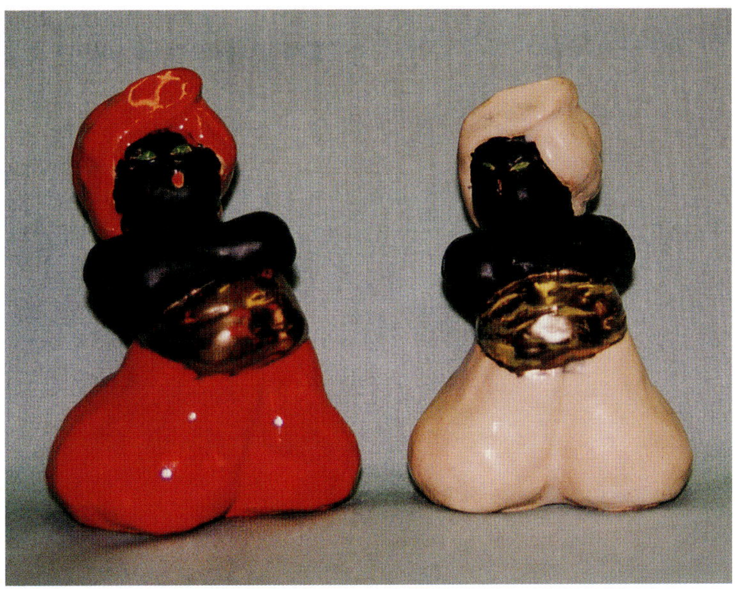

Genies. 4". $30-35.

Sheik and camel. 2.5". $18-20.

Sheik and harem girl. 3.75". $20-25.

People of the World

Amish couple.
3.25". $18-20.

Children. 3.5". $30-35.

Musician. 4". $40-45.

Mother and child. 4.25". $35-40.

Eskimo and igloo. 3.25". $18-20.

European couple. 3". $18-20.

Middle Eastern people. 2.5". $18-20.

Irish couple. 3". $18-20.

Mexican boy. 3".
Single. $15-18 pair.

Mexican and
donkey. 3". $15-18.

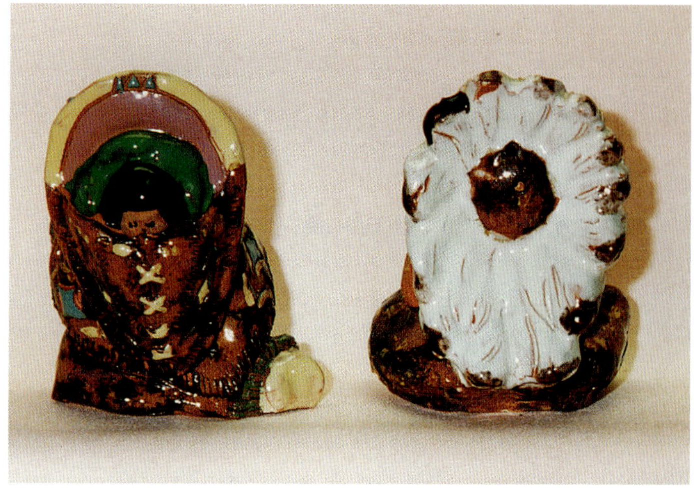

Native American couple. 3". $20-25. Front and back views.

Native American chief and wife. 3". $18-20.

Mother and child. 2.75". $20-25.

War dancers. 4.25". $20-25.

Natives. 5.5". $40-45.

Native and palm tree. 3.5". $35-40.

Natives. 4.75". $40-45.

Oriental ladies. 3". $25-30. Front and back views.

Oriental lady and bonsai tree. 2.25". $40-45.

Oriental couple. 4". $25-30.

Oriental lady and child. 3.75". $25-30.

People

Children's heads. 1". $12-15.

Babies. 2.25". $12-15.

Children in nightgowns. 2". $12-15.

Girl. 2.25". Single. $12-15 pair.

Girl at school. 2.5". $15-18.

Children. 3.25". $12-15.

Bunny children. 3". $12-15.

Girls with muffs. 3". $15-18.

Boy and sled. 2.25". $12-15.

"Big brother is watching." 3.5". $18-20.

Girl on pillow. 3.5". $12-15.

Graduates. 3.5". $12-15.

Gay '90s couple. 3.5". $18-20.

Ma and Pa. 2.5". $12-15.

"Gossiping over the Fence." 3". $18-20.

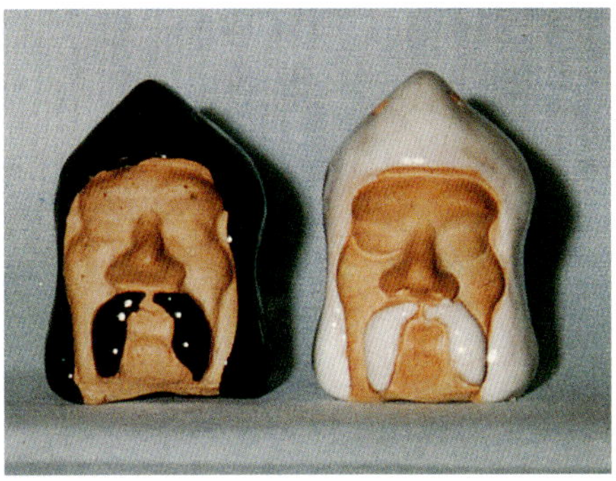

Heads. 1.5". $10-12.

"The Handout." 3.75". $18-20.

Man. 3". Single. $12-15 pair.

Lady. 3.5". Single.
$12-15 pair.

Ladies. 3.5". $12-15.

Sports

Cheerleaders. 3.25". $15-18.

Baseball players. 3.75". $18-20.

Football players. 4.75". $18-20.

Football players. 3.5". $18-20.

Umpires. 4.5". $18-20.

Weight lifter. 4". $15-18.

Miscellaneous

Bookworms. 2". $15-18.

Drip and drop. 3". $10-12.

Ark. 2.75". $12-15.

Totem poles. 3.5". $15-18.

Castle. 2.75". $18-20. One piece.

Card people. 3.25". $15-18.

Rose and rosebud. 2.25". $10-12.

Girl in flower. 2.5". $12-15. Stacker.

Flowers. 2". $10-12.

Acorns. 1.25". $12-15.

Legs with shoes. 3.75". $10-12.

Chariot. 2". Single. $12-15 pair.

Windmills. 3.25". $12-15.

Billee Vier

Billee Vier was a ceramist in the 1940s and early 1950s, when she apparently turned to painting and became recognized as an artist in the U.S. and other countries. She passed away about three years ago. Among items in her estate auction were several boxes of her salt and pepper shakers, which have been surfacing at antique shows and on Internet auctions. Shown below are the Billee Vier mark and a Ronald Vier mark. We do not know their relationship, but the printing is the same.

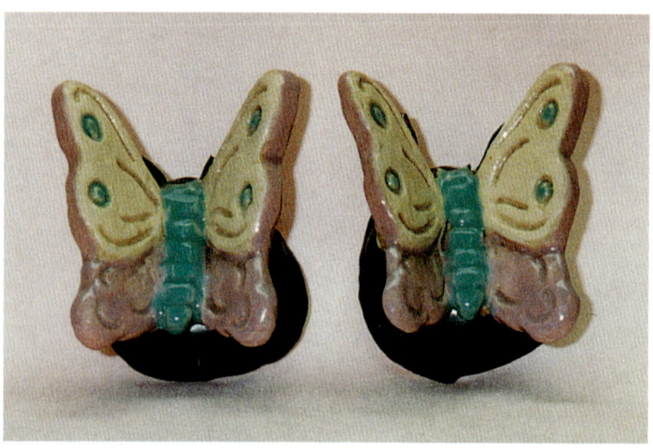

Butterflies. 1.5". $18-20.

Ducks. 5". $20-25.

Turtles. 1". $15-18.

Swans. 1.5". $12-15.

Fish. 2". $20-25.

Cat heads. 2.5". $20-25.

Tropical birds. 4.5". $30-35.

Boy. 5.5". Single. $25-30 pair.

Squirrels. 2.5". $20-25.

Boy. 2.25". Single. $25-30 pair.

Choir boys. 4". $35-40.

Lady with milking stool. 4.75". Single. $35-40 pair.

Sailor and girl. 3". $35-40.

Bride and groom. 4.5". $35-40.

Bride at altar. 3.75". $40-45. Together and apart.

Ladies. 5.75". Singles. $40-45 pair.
Lady on left has unglazed face.

Lady with fan. 4". $35-40.

Cowboys. 5". $35-40.

Couple. 6.5". $40-45.

Mexican couple. 8". $40-45.

Surfer girl. 6". $40-45. Together and apart.

Cheerleader. 4.75". $35-40.

Lady with bonnet. 4". $55-60.
Front and back views.

Boy and drum. 4". $35-40.

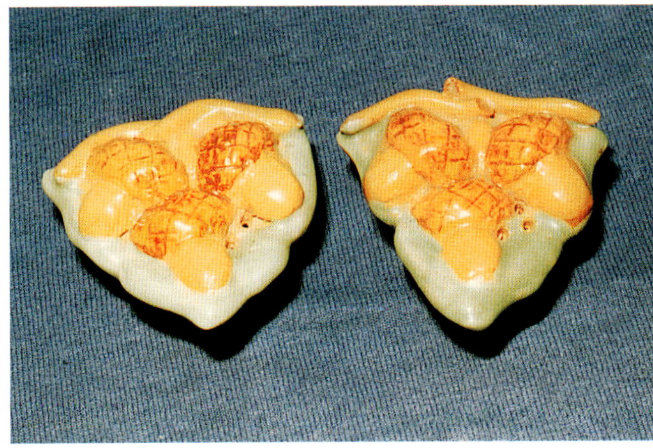

Acorns. 1.25". $12-15.

Oriental baskets. 2". $8-10.

Egg baskets. 2". $10-12.

Fruit baskets. 1". $12-15.

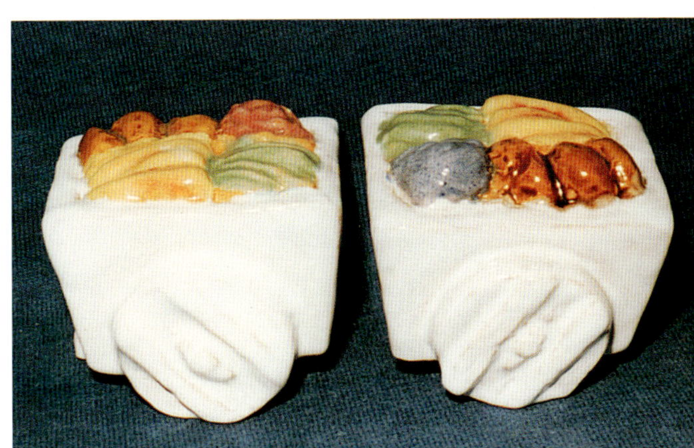

Fruit carts. 2". $12 15.

Church. 4.5". $35-40. One piece.

Mission. 4". $35-40.
One piece.

Lighthouse. 5". $35-40. Stacker.

Pine cones. 2". $15-18. One piece.

Daisies. 1.5". $10-12.

Sphinx. 3". $25-30. One piece. Front and side views.

Fans. .5". Probably singles. $10-12.

Shirley

These shakers have a copyright mark (©) but the Library of Congress found no record from 1940 to the present. This copyright was therefore unrecorded or recorded prior to 1940. To date, most shakers have been found by California collectors, leading us to believe this is another California pottery.

Bears. 3". $18-20.

Bears. 3". $18-20. Front and back views.

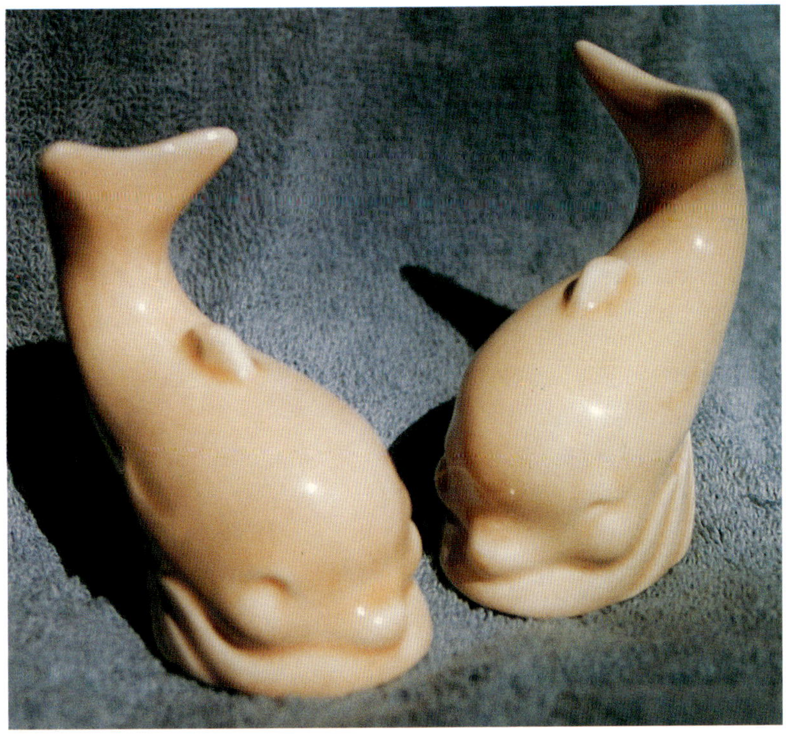

Dolphins. 3". $30-35.

Donkey. 2". $20-25. One piece. Front and back views.

Seahorses. 3.5". $25-30.

Horse heads. 3.25". $20-25.

Mary, Mary Quite Contrary.
3.25". $45-50.

Jack Spratt and wife. 4". $45-50. Together and apart.

Little Boy Blue. 2.25". $40-45.

Angels. 4". $25-30.

Bullfighters. 3.5". $30-35.

Cowboys. 4". $30-35.

Dutch couple. 3.25". $20-25.

Heralders. 4.5". $40 45.

Hawaiian couple.
3.5". $30-35.

Mexican and palm tree.
2.75". $25-30.

Navajo couple. 3". $25-30. She has classic rolled hair.

Front and back views.

Spanish couple. 3.5". $25-30.

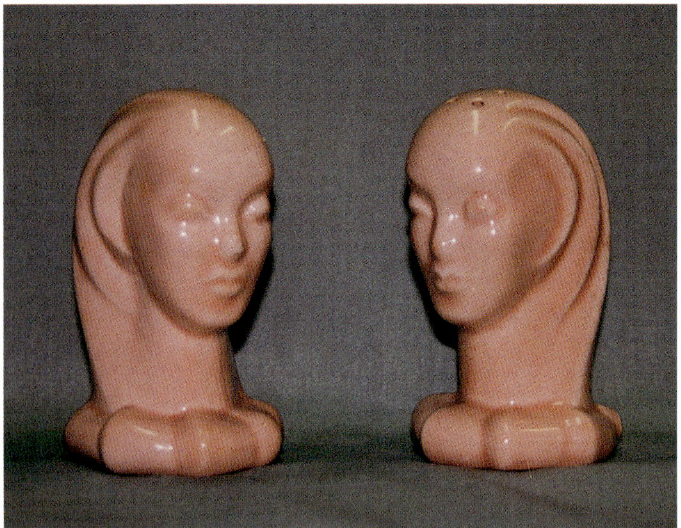

Classic lady heads. 3.25". $20-25. White glaze over reddish brown clay.

Classic lady heads. 3.25". $20-25.

Fisherman and fish. 3.25". $35-40.

Fisherman single. 3.25". $35-40 pair.

Sailors. 3.5". $25-30 pair. Front and back views.

Southern couple. 3.5". $40-45.

Singles.

Leyden Arts

We have not located any information about this company. However, some of the shakers are marked Leyden Arts, California so it obviously was located there. All sets have one and two holes, and are usually one solid color, although are occasionally found in two colors.

Giraffes. 5". $20-25.

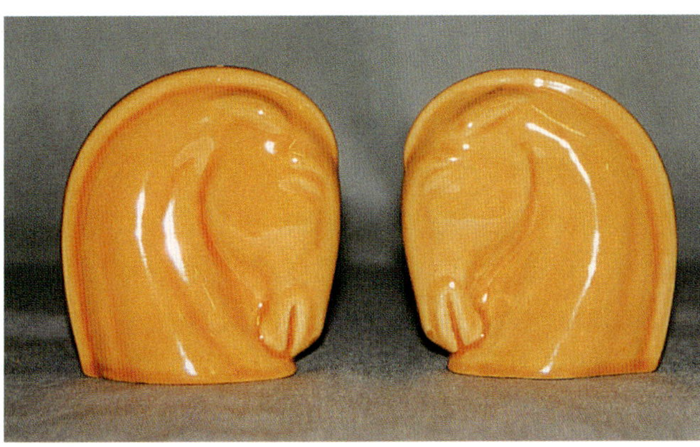

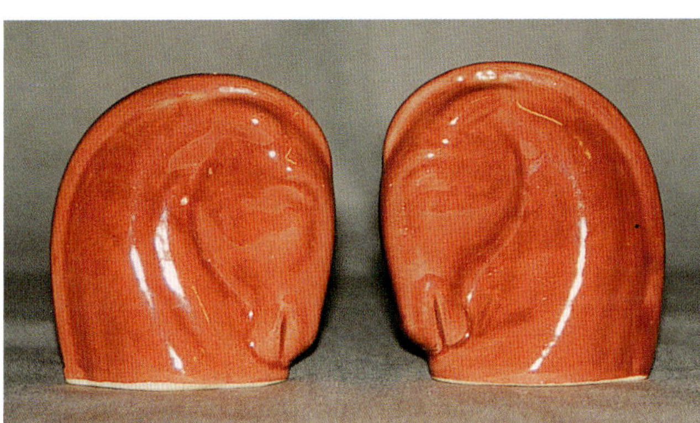

Horse heads. 3". $8-10.

Leaping fish. 3". $10-12.

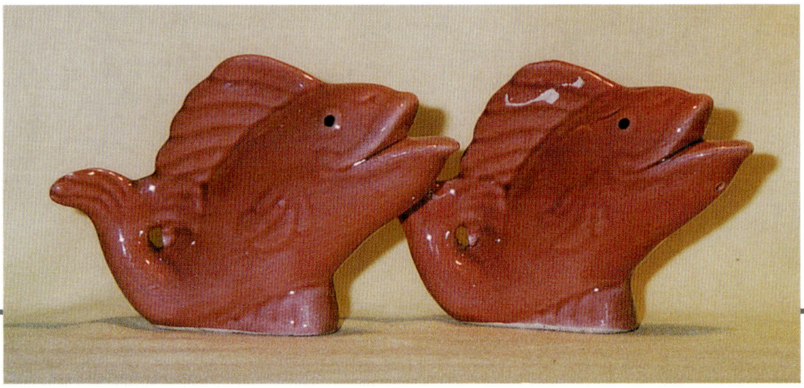

Peacocks. 2.75". $8-10.

Seahorses. 4". $12-15.

Seahorses. 4". $12-15.

Pelicans. 3". $10-12.

Pelicans. 3". $10-12.

San Juan Capistrano bells. 3". $10-12. Front and back views.

Sailing ships. 3". $10-12.

Sailing ships. 3". $10-12.

Bibliography

Chipman, Jack. *Collector's Encyclopedia of California Pottery*. Second Edition. Paducah KY: Collector Books, 1995.

Conti, Steve, A. DeWane Bethany, and Bill Seay. *Collector's Encyclopedia of Sascha Brastoff*. Paducah KY: Collector Books, 1995.

Huxford, Sharon, and Bob Huxford. *Schroeder's Antiques Price Guide*. Eighteenth Edition. Paducah KY: Collector Books, 2000.

Lehner, Lois. *Lehner's Encyclopedia of U.S. Marks on Pottery, Porcelain and Clay*. Paducah KY: Collector Books, 1988.

MSN Communities, Matthew Adams Pottery website: http://communities.msn.com/matthewadamspottery

MORE SCHIFFER TITLES

www.schifferbooks.com

America's Salt & Pepper Shakers. Sylvia Tompkins and Irene Thornburg. Found in a seemingly endless variety of shapes and styles, salt and pepper shakers have great collector appeal and are easy to display and enjoy! While interest has been steadily growing in American-made salt and pepper shakers, little has been written before on these charming and colorful "homegrown" collectibles. Now two well-known authors are together to present more than 800 American-made sets from the 1930s to the 1960s, along with background information on the companies and artists that produced them. Shown in over 650 color photos are shaker sets made by Rosemeade and Messer, sets from more than ten California potteries, and several never-before-seen sets from Ceramic Arts Studios. The authors provide helpful information on marks, labels, and other means of identification, and the captions include descriptions, heights, and values. A must for every salt and pepper shaker enthusiasts' library!

Size: 8 1/2" x 11" | 655 color photos | 160pp.
Price Guide
ISBN: 0-7643-1126-3 | soft cover | $29.95

Collecting Salt & Pepper Shaker Series. Irene Thornburg. This is the most comprehensive guide to salt and pepper shaker series ever published. Never before have so many shaker series been pictured in one book. Shown in full color are more than 850 sets, making up more than 125 series. Included are well-known names such as Rosemeade, Ceramic Arts, Lefton, Enesco, and more. This will be an indispensable reference book for both beginning and longtime collectors who have always wondered which sets "belong" together. Measurements, manufacturers, countries, and current values are provided. If you have never had an interest in salt and pepper shakers before, this book will open your eyes to a wonderful collectible!

Size: 6" x 9" | 361 color photos | 144pp.
Price Guide
ISBN: 0-7643-0493-3 | soft cover | $19.95

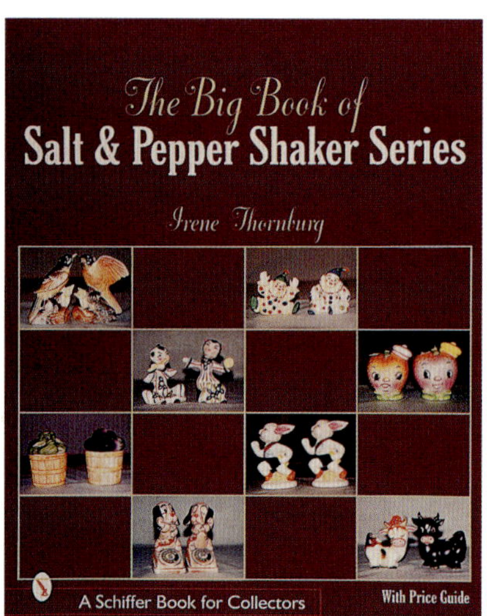

The Big Book of Salt and Pepper Shaker Series. Irene Thornburg. Calling all salt and pepper shaker enthusiasts! Containing almost 700 pictures, this captivating book features over 1,000 salt and pepper shaker sets comprising more than 225 series. The author illustrates a wide variety of series with three sets or more. Separate chapters highlight the World of Nature, Flowers, Fruit and Vegetables, People, and more. Included are many well-known manufacturers and importers such as Holt Howard, Napco, Norcrest, Lefton, Enesco, Vandor, and Clay Art. Measurements and current values are given. If you are looking for a wonderful collectible, this book will show you where to begin.

Size: 8 1/2" x 11" | 690 color photos | 160pp.
Price Guide
ISBN: 0-7643-0868-8 | soft cover | $29.95

1001 Salt & Pepper Shakers. Larry Carey & Sylvia Tompkins. An indispensible reference for anyone interested in salt and pepper shakers, compiled by two of America's foremost collectors. This book focuses on Black Americana, cat characters, mermaids, and Niagra Falls, with color photographs of over 1500 available items. A comprehensive guide, it includes color, size, and design variations of many pieces. A thorough price guide is provided to assist collectors on their hunts for these charming pieces.

Size: 8 1/2" x 11" 1500+ items in color 112pp.
Price Guide
ISBN: 0-88740-607-6 soft cover $19.95

1002 Salt and Pepper Shakers. Larry Carey & Sylvia Tompkins. This new volume focuses on nodder salt and pepper shakers with over 300 nodders as well as hundreds of early/discontinued Fitz and Floyd sets and Parkcraft sets, many of which have never before been shown in a book. All are shown in clear color photographs.This comprehensive guide includes for each set its identification, color, size, and design variations. A price guide is provided.

Size: 0-88740-789-7 soft cover $19.95
Price Guide
ISBN: 8 1/2" x 11" 500+ color photos 112pp.

1003 Salt & Pepper Shakers. Larry Carey & Sylvia Tompkins. This third volume by Larry Carey and Sylvia Tompkins focuses on character salt and pepper shakers. Featured in this book are popular television, movie, and cartoon characters. Also included are well-known mascots or symbols, such as the Loch Ness Monster and Smokey Bear. A large part of 1003 Salt & Pepper Shakers focuses on characters created by Walt Disney. The color, size, manufacturer, design variations, and value range for over 700 examples of character salt and pepper shakers is provided.

Size: 8 1/2" x 11" 300 color photos 176pp.
Value Guide
ISBN: 0-7643-0112-8 soft cover $29.95

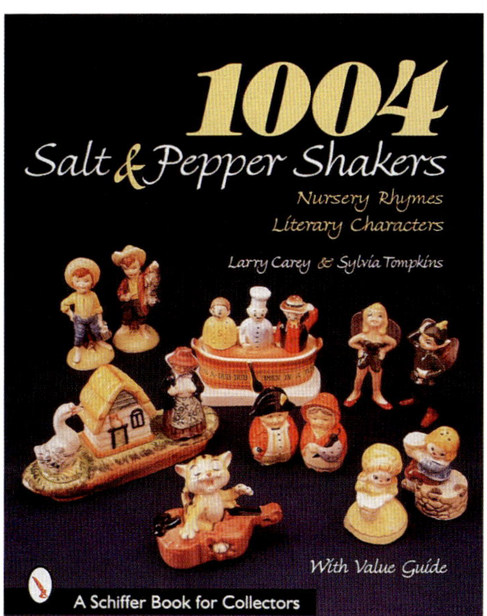

1004 Salt & Pepper Shakers. Larry Carey & Sylvia Tompkins. The increasingly collectible categories of nursery rhymes and literary characters, including children's stories and fables, provide the focus for this fourth book of salt and pepper shakers by experts Larry Carey and Sylvia Tompkins. This very popular area of salt and pepper shakers appeals to a wide range of collectors-it's the book for collectors who love classic literary characters such as those from Dickens, fairy tales, and Aesop's fables, to modern day characters such the Cat in the Hat and Curious George. Wonderful sets, from Aladdin and His Lamp to Wizards with Dragons, and everything in between (including series) are depicted in over 700 color photographs. A comprehensive guide, this book details each set's color, size, manufacturer, design variations, and value ranges along with licensing information as marked on the sets.

Size: 8 1/2" x 11" 700+ color photos 160pp.
Price Guide/Index
ISBN: 0-7643-0553-0 soft cover $29.95

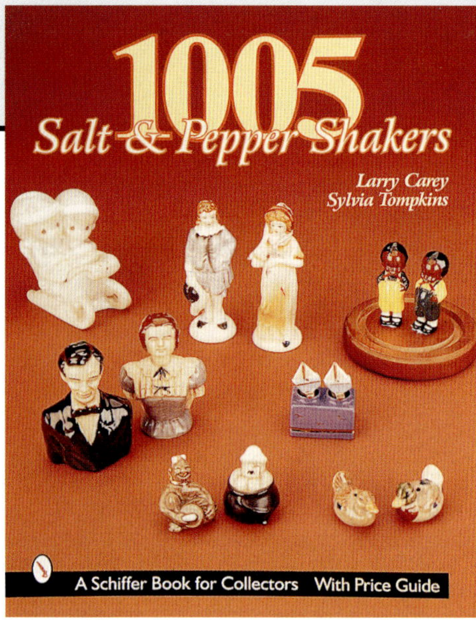

1005 Salt & Pepper Shakers. Larry Carey & Sylvia Tompkins. Here's another treasury of salt and pepper shakers from experts Larry Carey and Sylvia Tompkins! This fifth volume features a large assortment of darling miniatures, which make up a field of collecting all their own. The second chapter is devoted to famous personalities of all kinds, from Marilyn Monroe to Ghandi. The last part of the book presents shaker sets of charming company-developed characters like Holly Hobbie and Precious Moments. Here are the elements of a great price guide-full-color photography, specifications, and estimated values-brought to life in a book that's simply fun to look at. Whether you want to start a collection or continue building one, 1005 Salt & Pepper Shakers is a wonderful tool for your search!

Size: 8 1/2" x 11"	675 color photos	160pp.
Price Guide		
ISBN: 0-7643-0880-7	soft cover	$29.95

1006 Salt & Pepper Shakers: Advertising. Larry Carey & Sylvia Tompkins. Here is a field of salt and pepper shaker collecting all its own—advertising. A fascinating and diverse group of companies kept their logo within arm's reach at kitchen and dinner tables nationwide by customizing salt and pepper sets. In their sixth book, Larry Carey and Sylvia Tompkins have compiled a lively treasury of salt and pepper giveaways and gimmicks.This book features over 1,000 advertising sets in color photography. They are divided by subject, with chapters covering hotels and casinos, restaurants, entertainment, household products, food, beverages, foreign advertising, and many others. A fantastic chapter on transportation covers a wide selection of airline and gas station shakers. Full pricing information has been included for each set, with shakers ranging from the very common to the very rare. This book is an important resource for salt and pepper shaker collectors, and will appeal to collectors of all types of company advertising.

Size: 8 1/2" x 11"	1130 color photos	176pp.
Price Guide		
0-7643-1185-9	soft cover	$29.95

The Complete Salt and Pepper Shaker Book. Mike Schneider. The largest, most comprehensive and colorful guide to salt and pepper shakers ever published! A companion volume to The Complete Cookie Jar Book, published in 1991. The Complete Salt and Pepper Shaker Book shows more than 1600 sets of figural shakers in full color. The collection includes those by American potteries such as Rosemeade and Ceramic Arts Studio that have never appeared in a book before.Company histories, measurements of shakers, and pictures of marks and paper labels are among the book's innovative features. As some salt and pepper shakers currently attract hundreds of dollars, this book is a must for collectors, dealers, and appraisers. Look inside, even if you have never held an interest in salt and pepper shakers before, and this book will open your eyes to a wonderful collectible. A price guide is included.

Size: 9" x 12"	1600+ sets	252pp.
Price Guide		
ISBN: 0-88740-494-4	hard cover	$49.95